My World of ANIMALS™

SPIDERS

JANNELL KHU

The Rosen Publishing Group's
PowerKids Press™
New York

1

For Zachary Kopke, who loves Spiderman

Published in 2004 by The Rosen Publishing Group, Inc.
29 East 21st Street, New York, NY 10010

First Edition

Book Design: Mike Donnellan
Illustration by Mike Donnellan

Photo Credits: Cover, pp. 7, 9, 13 (right), 15 © David Liebman; p. 5 © Alan Morgan/Peter Arnold; p. 11 © Paul Freed/Animals Animals; p. 13 (left) © Carol Hughes; p. 17 © Robert Noonan; p. 19 © James Gerhholdt/Peter Arnold; p. 21 Robert and Linda Mitchell; p. 22 by Cindy Reiman.

Khu, Jannell
Spiders / Jannell Khu.
        p. cm. — (My world of animals)
Includes bibliographical references and index.
Summary: This book introduces spiders, describing their physical characteristics and their behavior.
ISBN 1-4042-2523-4 (lib.)
1. Spiders—Juvenile literature   [1. Spiders]   I. Title   II. Series
QL458.4.K48 2004   2003-010275
595.4'4—dc21

Manufactured in the United States of America

CONTENTS

A spider is a type of animal. Spiders have eight legs and two body parts. The front part of the spider is the head and the back part is the body.

4

5

Spiders can look different from one another. Spiders can be different shapes, sizes, and colors.

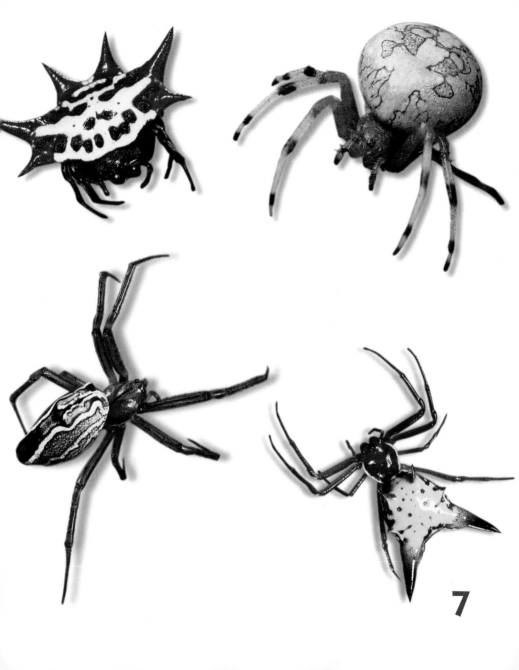

7

This spider is white. It is hard to see the spider against the white flower. This keeps the spider safe.

9

This spider is about the size of a coin. There are spiders that are smaller than a coin. There are spiders that are bigger than a coin.

11

Some spiders are so big that they can catch a fish or a frog for their meal!

13

Spiders shoot out thread from their bodies. The thread is called silk. Silk is coming out of this spider's body.

14

15

Spiders use silk to make webs. Not all webs look alike. Some webs are messy and some are neat.

17

Spiders use their webs to catch bugs for food. Spiders eat bugs such as ants and grasshoppers.

19

Some spiders make webs so that they can rest and hide. This spider waits to catch a bug for its meal. There are many kinds of spiders and many kinds of webs.

21

WORDS TO KNOW

coin

grasshopper

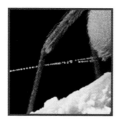

thread

web

Here are more books to read about spiders:

Fishing Spiders
by Jake Miller
Rosen Publishing Group

Spiders!
by Chris Graham
Rosen Publishing Group

Due to the changing nature of Internet links, PowerKids Press has developed an online list of Web sites related to the subject of this book. This site is updated regularly. Please use this link to access the list:

www.powerkidslinks.com/mwanim/spider/

INDEX

Word Count: 198

Note to Parents, Teachers, and Librarians

PowerKids Readers are specially designed to help emergent and beginning readers build their skills in reading for information. Simple vocabulary and concepts are paired with real-life photographs or stunning, detailed images from the natural world. Readers will respond to written language by linking meaning with their own everyday experiences and observations. Sentences are short and simple, employing a basic vocabulary of sight words, as well as new words that describe objects or processes that take place in the natural world. Large type, clean design, and photographs corresponding directly to the text all help children to decipher meaning. Features such as a contents page, picture glossary, and index help children to get the most out of PowerKids Readers. They also introduce children to the basic elements of a book, which they will encounter in their future reading experiences. Lists of related books and Web sites encourage kids to explore other sources and to continue the process of learning.